THE FUNNIEST CRICKET QUOTES... EVER!

Also available

The Funniest Football Quotes... Ever!
The Funniest Tennis Quotes... Ever!
The Funniest Chelsea Quotes... Ever!
The Funniest Liverpool Quotes... Ever!
The Funniest West Ham Quotes... Ever!
The Funniest Spurs Quotes... Ever!
The Funniest Arsenal Quotes... Ever!
The Funniest Man City Quotes... Ever!
The Funniest Newcastle Quotes... Ever!
The Funniest United Quotes... Ever!
The Funniest Leeds Quotes... Ever!
The Funniest Boro Quotes... Ever!
The Funniest Forest Quotes... Ever!
The Funniest Sunderland Quotes... Ever!
The Funniest Leicester Quotes... Ever!
The Funniest Saints Quotes... Ever!
The Funniest Everton Quotes... Ever!
The Funniest Villa Quotes... Ever!
The Funniest QPR Quotes... Ever!
The Funniest England Quotes... Ever!

Copyright © 2022 by Eagle Books.

No part of this publication may be reproduced, stored in a retrieval system or transmitted in any form by any means, electronic, mechanical, photocopying, or otherwise, without prior written permission of the publisher Eagle Books.

contact@gmediagroup.co.uk

Printed in Europe and the USA

ISBN: 978-1-917744-17-1
Imprint: Eagle Books

Photos courtesy of: shutterstock.com/g/clintp; shutterstock.com/g/alabony.

Contents

Game For A Laugh..7

Say That Again?...17

Verbal Volleys...27

Media Circus...43

Player Power...49

Field Of Dreams...63

Talking Balls..73

Off The Pitch...87

Pundit Paradise...97

THE FUNNIEST CRICKET QUOTES... EVER!

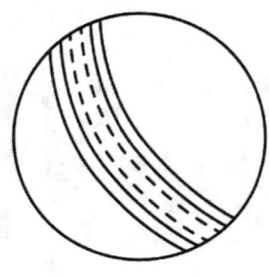

GAME FOR A LAUGH

THE FUNNIEST CRICKET QUOTES... EVER!

"I only really have one problem with the World Test Championship and that's how the hell are you meant to drink out of a mace?"
Jimmy Neesham on New Zealand's latest trophy

"Pakistan is the sort of place every man should send his mother-in-law to, for a month, all expenses paid."
Ian Botham

"It looks more suitable for growing carrots."
Andy Atkinson, ICC grounds inspector, on Bermuda's new pitch

Game For A Laugh

"I don't want to put too much emphasis on it, in case they send me back there."

South Africa's Alviro Petersen on the value of first-class cricket

"Clinching the [County] Championship is a strange sensation... There's more atmosphere in a doctor's waiting room."

Simon Hughes

"You still want to kill each other on the field, and have a beer and a chat about hair off the field."

Jacques Kallis on mingling with rival players at Twenty20 franchise tournaments

THE FUNNIEST CRICKET QUOTES... EVER!

"I don't know an England player who could fix a light bulb, let alone a match."

Darren Gough

"I am happy [England] gave us the game of cricket, which they can't play very well, and the English language, which I can't speak very well."

Former India captain Kapil Dev

"You can't exactly put a fielder in the car park, can you?"

Ravi Bopara on setting a field for Chris Gayle

Game For A Laugh

"I remember when someone asked me for my autograph, and when I went over, they slapped a minced beef and onion pie on my head."

Phil Tufnell on playing cricket in Australia

"Diaper and five-day cricket should only be changed when they are soiled."

Virender Sehwag reckons the idea of four-day Tests stinks

"And my tip to all bowlers – learn to bat! Bowling is for mugs."

Kevin Pietersen

THE FUNNIEST CRICKET QUOTES... EVER!

"I've done the elephant. I've done the poverty. I might as well go home."

Phil Tufnell on touring in India

"The first rule of batting is to use your bat."

Faf du Plessis

"We used to get a drinks list after a game. Now you get an ice bath."

Andrew Flintoff on changes in the game

"We didn't have anti-perspirants back then."

Sunil Gavaskar on a lack of team huddles in his day

Game For A Laugh

"I get asked, 'What's better, hitting a six or having sex?' I don't hit that many sixes. If I had to wait that long between stints in the sack, my life wouldn't be too great."
Andrew Strauss

"Sometimes people think it's like polo, played on horseback, and I remember one guy thought it was a game involving insects."
West Indies and USA international Clayton Lambert on explaining cricket to Americans

"I'm a big believer that the coach is something you travel in to get to and from the game."
Shane Warne is not a fan of coaching

THE FUNNIEST CRICKET QUOTES... EVER!

"Being on 99 has the habit of turning sane men into idiots. I said, 'Sorry mate' and told him I was an idiot."

Andrew Strauss on a bad call which led to Ian Bell's run-out

"It is like giving a machine gun to a monkey: it can be fantastic or it can be an absolute disaster, too."

England boss Hugh Morris on cricketers using Twitter

"Helmets are unfair to bowlers."

Viv Richards

Game For A Laugh

"Closest sport in America is baseball. But cricket lasts five days. We break every now and then for food. And we spend a lot of time rubbing our balls on our trousers."

Andrew Flintoff explains cricket to singer Jennifer Lopez

"They'd win the first four Tests and we'd try to nick one at the end when they were all drunk."

Nasser Hussain on Australia's era of dominance

"If we have an early exit, we'll have two weeks in Leicester. That won't be good for anybody."

Ricky Ponting

THE FUNNIEST CRICKET QUOTES... EVER!

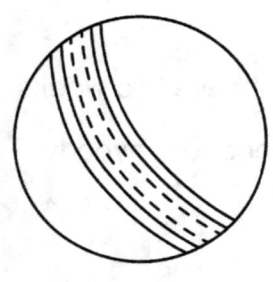

SAY THAT AGAIN?

THE FUNNIEST CRICKET QUOTES... EVER!

"I might as well have been speaking to the vicar about gangsta rap."

Kevin Pietersen on explaining his IPL commitments to Andrew Strauss

"We have had exceptionally wet weather in Derby – everywhere in the country is in the same boat."

Kenya CEO Tom Sears

"I have enjoyed when a gorgeous cricket ball declines the advances of my well-manicured cricket bat. But loaded with the perseverance of a sincere lover, my bat wins."

Gautam Gambhir

Say That Again?

"If we can beat South Africa on Saturday that would be a great fillip in our cap."

Graham Gooch

"We didn't have metaphors in our day. We didn't beat around the bush."

Fred Trueman

"They're very experienced Test players with a lot of caps under them."

Duncan Fletcher

"We've won one on the trot."

Alec Stewart

THE FUNNIEST CRICKET QUOTES... EVER!

"I absolutely insist that all my boys are in bed before breakfast."

Captain Colin Ingleby-Mackenzie on how Hampshire won the County Championship

"I presented my trousers to the committee; I had nothing to hide."

Mike Atherton

"It was as if he still writes to Santa Claus and puts a tooth under his pillow for the tooth fairy."

Kevin Pietersen on Alastair Cook refusing to believe the @kpgenius Twitter parody account was run by an England player

Say That Again?

"The only way to maintain a winning streak is to keep winning. Not by losing."

Quinton de Kock

"My cricket's all been played in a triangle of about two or three square miles."

Phil Carrick

"I think we are all slightly down in the dumps after another loss. We may be in the wrong sign... Venus may be in the wrong juxtaposition with somewhere else."

Ted Dexter

THE FUNNIEST CRICKET QUOTES... EVER!

"I'll come for a lamb rogan josh and a pint."

Andrew Flintoff tweets his IPL "reserve price" to Kevin Pietersen as "an old all-rounder who can't bat and [is] too unfit to bowl"

"It's a catch-21 situation."

Kevin Pietersen on missing a 2005 tour to Sri Lanka

"When things are going well, the toothbrush bristles stay straight and soft. When it isn't, it seems the toothbrush has the-out-of-the-bed look."

Gautam Gambhir

Say That Again?

"If my grandfather was alive, he would have slaughtered a cow."

South Africa's Makhaya Ntini after taking 5-75 against England at Lord's

"A fart competing with thunder."

Graham Gooch in Australia, in 1990-91

"One-day cricket is like fast food. No one wants to cook."

Viv Richards

"I'll take an ugly 100 over a pretty 10 any day."

Alastair Cook

THE FUNNIEST CRICKET QUOTES... EVER!

"I forgot to pack enough undies, so I fashioned some briefs from a flowery lampshade and two Mars bar wrappers. Very D&G."
Graeme Swann

"People will be surprised by this, but I'm actually very scared of the dark."
Andrew Flintoff

"This achievement we have achieved is a great achievement."
Michael Vaughan on victory over the West Indies

Say That Again?

"For some strange reason, my hands have gone outside my eyes."
Kevin Pietersen

"I gave the chewing gum such a workout. I am disappointed that no one approached me for advertising. I did the chewing gum a world of good, it was like my brother."
Viv Richards

"Sorry, skipper, a leopard can't change its stripes."
Lennie Pascoe

THE FUNNIEST CRICKET QUOTES... EVER!

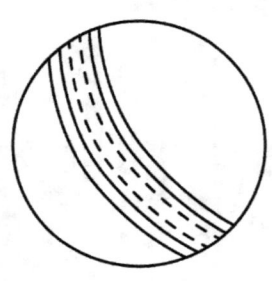

VERBAL VOLLEYS

THE FUNNIEST CRICKET QUOTES... EVER!

"Hell, Gatt, move out of the way, I can't see the stumps."

Dennis Lillee, stopping in mid-run, treats Mike Gatting to a spot of verbals

Australia's Ian Healy: "You're a f*cking cheat."
Mike Atherton: "When in Rome, dear boy."

Viv Richards: "This is my island, my culture. Don't you be staring at me. In my culture we just bowl."
Merv Hughes [after he dismissed the batsman]: "In my culture we just say f*ck off."

Verbal Volleys

"Now which of you b*stards called this b*stard a b*stard?"
England captain Douglas Jardine to his Australian counterpart Bill Woodfull

"No good hitting me there, mate, there's nothing to damage."
Derek Randall to Dennis Lillee after being struck on the head by a bouncer

Javed Miandad: "You fat bus conductor!"
Merv Hughes [after he dismissed him a few balls later]: "Tickets please!"

THE FUNNIEST CRICKET QUOTES... EVER!

Ian Botham: "I know you think I'm great Hoggy, but no need to get down on your knees."

After Rodney Hogg lost his balance while bowling and fell at Botham's feet

Craig McDermott: "You've got to bat on this in a minute, Tuffers. Hospital food suit you?"

After getting bowled by Phil Tufnell

Dennis Lillee: "I can see why you are batting so badly, you've got some sh*t on the end of your bat."

[The batsman inspects the bottom of his bat].

Lillee: "Wrong end, mate."

Verbal Volleys

Rod Marsh: "So how's your wife and my kids?"
Ian Botham: "The wife's fine, but the kids are retarded."

"If we don't beat you, we'll knock your bloody heads off."
England fast bowler Bill Voce to Vic Richardson in the Bodyline series

Greg Thomas [Describing the ball]: "It's red, round and weighs about five ounces, in case you were wondering."
Viv Richards [After hitting the ball out of the ground]: "You know what it looks like, now you go and find it."

THE FUNNIEST CRICKET QUOTES... EVER!

Glenn McGrath: "Hey Eddo, why are you so f*cking fat?"

Eddo Brandes: "Because every time I f*ck your mother, she throws me a biscuit."

Shane Warne: "I've been waiting two years for another chance to humiliate you."

Daryll Cullinan: "Looks like you spent it eating."

"Mind the windows, Tino."

Freddie Flintoff to Tino Best... before Tino was stumped while trying to thump Ashley Giles into the pavilion

Verbal Volleys

Steve Waugh: "Oh, I get it. Nobody's talking to Steve. OK! I'll talk to my f*cking self!"
After realising England wouldn't sledge him

Merv Hughes: "You can't f*cking bat!"
Robin Smith [after he whacked him to the boundary]: "Hey Merv, we make a fine pair. I can't f*cking bat & you can't f*cking bowl."

"You don't get a runner for being an overweight, unfit, fat c*nt!"
Ian Healy to Arjuna Ranatunga after he called for a runner on a hot night

THE FUNNIEST CRICKET QUOTES... EVER!

Glenn McGrath: "So what does Brian Lara's d*ck taste like?"

Ramnaresh Sarwan: "I don't know. Ask your wife."

McGrath: "If you ever f*cking mention my wife again, I'll f*cking rip your f*cking throat out."

Mark Waugh: "F*ck me, look who it is. Mate, what are you doing out here, there's no way you're good enough to play for England."

James Ormond: "Maybe not, but at least I'm the best player in my family."

"Get ready for a broken f*cking arm."

Michael Clarke to James Anderson

Verbal Volleys

Malcolm Marshall: "Now David [Boon], are you going to get out now or am I going to have to bowl around the wicket and kill you?"

"Take a good look at this a*se of mine, you'll see plenty of it this summer."
David Steele to Rodney Marsh

Mark Waugh: "Oh, I remember you from a couple years ago in Australia. You were sh*t then, you're f*cking useless now."

Adam Parore: "Yeah, that's me and when I was there you were going out with that old, ugly sl*t and now I hear you've married her. You dumb c*nt."

THE FUNNIEST CRICKET QUOTES... EVER!

"You are not God, you are a cricketer, and I'm a better one."

Kevin Pietersen to India's Yuvraj Singh

"I'll walk you to the changing room. What are you averaging? You must know your average? 9? 10? Maybe 9.5, so we'll give you 10."

Mark Boucher to Zimbabwe's Tatenda Taibu

Ian Healy: "Put a Mars Bar on a good length. That should do it."

The wicket keeper's advice to Shane Warne to get the portly Sri Lanka batsman Arjuna Ranatunga out of his crease

Verbal Volleys

Steve Waugh to Ricky Ponting: "Go to field right under Nasser Hussain's nose."

Ian Healy: "That could be anywhere inside a three-mile radius."

Jamie Siddons to Steve Waugh after he casually strolled to the crease: "For f*ck's sake, it's not a f*cking Test match."

Waugh: "Of course it's not, you're here."

Raman Subba Row [after a ball travels through him at slip]: "I should've kept my legs together, Fred."

Fred Trueman: "So should your mother."

THE FUNNIEST CRICKET QUOTES... EVER!

"Don't bother shutting it son, you will be back soon."

Fred Trueman to an Australian batsman entering the field

Tony Greig: "When are your balls going to drop, sonny?"

David Hookes: "I don't know, but at least I'm playing cricket for my own country."

"I'll bowl you a f*cking piano. Let's see if you can play that!"

Merv Hughes bowling to Graham Gooch, who kept playing and missing

Verbal Volleys

"I don't mind this lot (the Australian slips cordon) chirping at me, but you're just the bus driver."
Nasser Hussain to Justin Langer

"All you Aussies are a bunch of hicks who do not know anything about cricket."
Ian Botham

Phil Tufnell: "What, are you blind?"
Umpire: "I beg your pardon!"
Tufnell: "Are you deaf as well?"

"You are a damned lot of sneaks."
WG Grace to Australia players at The Oval

THE FUNNIEST CRICKET QUOTES... EVER!

"What do you think this is, a f*cking tea party? No you can't have a f*cking glass of water. You can f*cking wait like all the rest of us."

Allan Border to England batsman Robin Smith

"Mate, if you just turn the bat over, you'll find instructions on the other side."

Merv Hughes to Robin Smith after the batsman repeatedly played and missed

Ian Healy: "Got your legs shaking?"
Arjuna Ranatunga: "Yes, I'm tired after sleeping with your wife."

Verbal Volleys

"Tap that one down you little b*stard."

Tony Lock bowls a bouncer at Richie Benaud after a long period of gardening

"Try hitting that for six."

Merv Hughes to Hansie Cronje after farting loudly

"Go and deflate yourself, you balloon."

Daryll Cullinan to Shane Warne

"You convicts are all the same."

Malcolm Marshall to Steve Waugh after he refused to walk

THE FUNNIEST CRICKET QUOTES... EVER!

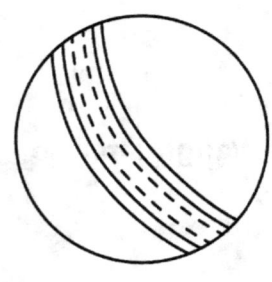

MEDIA CIRCUS

THE FUNNIEST CRICKET QUOTES... EVER!

"I am not talking to anyone in the British media... they are all pr*cks."

Australia captain Allan Border at a press conference at Hove

Reporter: "Why do international cricketers play so many matches?"

Alec Stewart: "They do it to pay your wages."

Q: "What can England take away from the third day's play?"

Ben Stokes: "A bit of sunburn, probably, to be honest."

After England were frustrated by India's batting

Media Circus

Reporter: "Do you feel that the selectors and yourself have been vindicated by the result?"

Mike Gatting: "I don't think the press are vindictive. They can write what they want."

"He's a pr*ck. He's a f*cking pr*ck. He sits there making judgments about players that are much better than he ever was. Believe me, he's a pr*ck."

Andrew Flintoff launches stinging attack on pundit Mike Atherton

Q: "What was Chris Gayle thinking?"

Darren Sammy: "I'm not Jesus Christ! I don't know what's going on in his mind."

THE FUNNIEST CRICKET QUOTES... EVER!

"One of (Kevin) Pietersen's great triumphs this week was that he managed to get the assortment of drunks, cynics, skivers, scoundrels, gamblers and geeks collectively known as the press corps buzzing with excitement."
Mike Atherton on the press pack

"What a pleasure being able to bowl bouncers at journos today!! Managed a few bruises!"
Stuart Broad gets payback

Interviewer: "Daryll, who are your favourite actors?"
Daryll Cullinan: "Dustin Hoffman and some Aussie bowlers in the act of appealing."

Media Circus

Commentator Ramiz Raja: "Is it money or passion that fuels your game?"

Shoaib Malik: "Ramiz, they don't ask such tough questions even in an American visa interview."

Reporter: "What's the best sledge you have faced?"

Mark Butcher: [After a long pause] "Sorry, but I really can't think of any that are suitable for the Guardian – most have been fairly obscene."

"I can still handle ten guys like you alone."
Shahid Afridi lauds his fitness to a reporter

THE FUNNIEST CRICKET QUOTES... EVER!

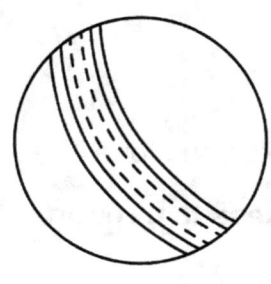

PLAYER POWER

THE FUNNIEST CRICKET QUOTES... EVER!

"I can't really say I'm batting badly. I'm not batting long enough to be batting badly."
Greg Chappell

"I have prepared for the worst-case scenario, but it could be even worse than that."
Monty Panesar

"I always walked… bit hard to stand there with all three stumps lying on the ground."
Glenn McGrath

"I'd have looked even faster in colour."
Fred Trueman

Player Power

"I've been a bit of a useless tosser up to now."
Paul Collingwood

"I don't really see myself as a cricketer. I see myself as quite a cultured person."
Adam Zampa

"In Australia they think I'm Stephen Hawking."
Andrew Flintoff on presenting an Aussie current affairs programme

"After I've played a shot, I switch off, maybe think about sex and get ready to go again."
Ricky Ponting

THE FUNNIEST CRICKET QUOTES... EVER!

"I have to fight bowlers in Jupiter, Mars and in all these places now. So, I am the Universe Boss, always."
Chris Gayle is out of this world

"I'm very proud of my fitness record. Jimmy Anderson told me to drink a glass of cement to toughen up."
Alastair Cook

"You are a jerk! I averaged 2."
Glenn Maxwell replies to a fan's tweet which said he averaged one in the New Zealand ODIs

Player Power

Q: "Do you remember your first series as ODI captain against Sri Lanka?"
Alastair Cook: "I was called a donkey, wasn't I? So, yes."

"I have been known to bite myself, bite my hand."
New Zealand's Mitchell McClenaghan on getting motivated

"There's a bit of pressure on me now if anything electrically goes wrong in the dressing room."
Former electrician and England opener Michael Carberry

THE FUNNIEST CRICKET QUOTES... EVER!

"You're always going to be criticised to a degree. Some people didn't like Mother Teresa as well."
Brendon McCullum

"In my first few games for England I would stand in the field for six-and-a-half hours absolutely cr*pping myself."
Matt Prior

"I wouldn't get in the Scotland team now. I told them that."
Paul Collingwood admits his T20 career is over

Player Power

"What am I going to do at the ground? Hold the players' hands and have a cup of tea with them?"

Ian Botham on why he doesn't need to watch the team play in his role as Durham chairman

"You can't smoke 20 a day and bowl fast."

Phil Tufnell on why he became a spinner

"My knee is fine, but my neck hurts from watching all the sixes hit by Australia."

Michael Vaughan at the 2007 T20 series

THE FUNNIEST CRICKET QUOTES... EVER!

"Take a bit of beer and manure and rub it on your forehead."

Jacques Kallis on the secret of his new head of hair

"I've never been one for stats and milestones, I just try to do the best for my team. I'm the third fastest person in the history of the game to get 10,000 runs."

Ricky Ponting

"I'm a fair dinkum pom."

Australia-raised Sam Hain declares for England

Player Power

"I'm ugly, I'm overweight, but I'm happy."

Andrew Flintoff

"Aussie sledging? I'm just glad they've heard of me!"

Monty Panesar

"I am 100 per cent method, 80 per cent skill and 150 per cent madness."

Mr 330 per cent Ravi Ashwin

"I'm not crazy, but I talk to myself. And sometimes I answer back."

Chris Gayle

THE FUNNIEST CRICKET QUOTES... EVER!

"I could bowl a heap of poo tomorrow."

Dale Steyn

"I'm only here for the food!"

Andrew Flintoff after being named joint ICC Player of the Year, 2005

"I sleep the whole day after breakfast to get in shape for the game."

Chris Gayle on his pre-match routine

"Can you make me look like Paul Newman?"

Sunil Gavaskar to a plastic surgeon after he had been hit in the jaw while fielding

Player Power

"Punching lockers isn't the way forward for anyone. There's only going to be one winner there."
Ben Stokes

"I can't bat, can't bowl and can't field these days. I've every chance of being picked for England."
Essex spinner Ray East

"It stinks. I got it out of the bag before. It was rancid."
Brendon McCullum on his cap before his 100th Test

THE FUNNIEST CRICKET QUOTES... EVER!

"I'm jealous of my parents. I'll never have a kid as cool as theirs."
Chris Gayle

"Gel is more macho than a hairband."
Wasim Akram

"With regard to the broken finger, when batting I'll just have to play it by ear."
Marcus Trescothick

"They came to see me bat, not you bowl."
WG Grace, putting the bails back on his stumps after being bowled first ball

Player Power

"I just want to get into the middle and get the right sort of runs."

Robin Smith, suffering from diarrhoea on an England tour of India

"It's far more daunting than bowling to Ricky Ponting or facing Shane Warne."

Andrew Flintoff on hearing he was to duet with Elton John

"I am Australian, as simple as that, and I always will be. I'm not going to be Adolf Warne or anything like that."

Shane Warne

THE FUNNIEST CRICKET QUOTES... EVER!

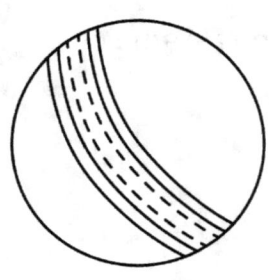

FIELD OF DREAMS

THE FUNNIEST CRICKET QUOTES... EVER!

"I am very happy and it will allow me to have a lot more rice."

Eoin Morgan after being awarded a rice cooker for being named Man of the Match in a Dhaka Premier Division game

"Many times I have cursed the rain in Manchester, but today I would take it home to meet my grandma and marry it."

Graeme Swann after the weather helped England out in the Ashes

"The wicket didn't do too much, but when it did, it did too much."

Mike Gatting

Field Of Dreams

"We were disappointed, but then Billy Bowden told us it was just cheese."

Dinesh Chandimal on the missile that hit a Sri Lanka player at Headingley

"To get one in that area is bad enough but to get two in a row is tough. He's talking to us in a high voice."

Sam Cook after Trent Rockets teammate Alex Hales was hit twice in the groin area by Reece Topley

"We finished third in a two-horse race."

Matt Prior on England's display against Australia

THE FUNNIEST CRICKET QUOTES... EVER!

"Chucking a beer over James Anderson's head? Whoopee doo. I once put a dead shark in Mike Atherton's bed."
Alan Mullally

"It was in the gents! That was nice, for my first meeting with the match referee."
Ashley Giles describes an awkward moment

"Some days you're the windscreen, some you're the bug."
Michael Hussey on a dropped catch that brought up his century against Sri Lanka

Field Of Dreams

"You know the song is coming – so I just sang 'Frozen' in my head! A happy song. Let it go..."
Mitchell Johnson on getting through the Barmy Army's chants about him

"If it had been a cheese roll, it would never have got past him."
Graham Gooch on Shane Warne's 'ball of the century' which bowled Mike Gatting

"The lads were checking their Euromillions numbers."
Joss Buttler on the codes being displayed from the England dressing room

THE FUNNIEST CRICKET QUOTES... EVER!

"We decided to put the foot on the pedal towards the end – and it came off."
Paul Collingwood

"The hardest part about the whole affair was that it took me a month to get the fake tan off my hand."
Simon Katich on clutching Michael Clarke by the throat in a dressing room row

"I'm regularly asked if I want a Flake with my 99, but I'd be disappointed if it was any different."
Alex Hales on getting out on 99, which stopped him from becoming England's first T20 centurion

Field Of Dreams

"I was checking the backs of my whites, making sure they weren't too brown. He was quite quick."

Brad Hogg on the first time he faced Brett Lee in a match

"My mother could've beaten me all over the place on that first morning at Brisbane."

Graeme Swann says he "bowled like a 12-year-old" during the first Test

"It was like watching Edward Scissorhands coping with a cricket ball coming down at him from a great height."

Monty Panesar on fielding a high catch

THE FUNNIEST CRICKET QUOTES... EVER!

"I just stood there and realised that it was the closest I've ever come to thinking I could willingly slap two guys on my own team."
Kevin Pietersen after Graeme Swann and Stuart Broad were laying into England's fielders

"Not seen that many wickets fall in a day's play since 1996 in my back garden... and at least that was a green seamer!!"
Stuart Broad after 16 wickets fell on the first day of the Test with Pakistan

"It's been hard to penetrate their batsmen."
Paul Collingwood

Field Of Dreams

"Quite why [Ricky Ponting] was blaming me when his partner, Damien Martyn, had called him for a suicidal single to cover, I don't know. You know what's more? All the palaver caused me to burn my toast."
Duncan Fletcher after substitute fielder Gary Pratt ran out the Aussie

"That was unplayable, just like the Spice Girls."
Shane Warne

"He said I looked like Tarzan, and wondered how I could bowl fast looking like that."
Shoaib Akhtar on Andrew Flintoff

THE FUNNIEST CRICKET QUOTES... EVER!

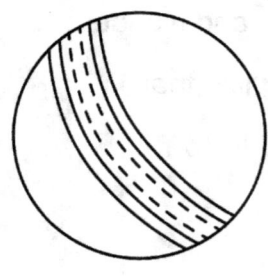

TALKING BALLS

THE FUNNIEST CRICKET QUOTES... EVER!

"I literally stayed up until 1.30 in the morning to watch him cry live on TV. What a pleasure that was."

Matt Prior on David Warner

"Geoff Boycott has the uncanny knack of being where fast bowlers aren't."

Tony Greig

"I just hope the Australian public give it to him [Stuart Broad] right from the word go for the whole summer and I hope he cries and he goes home."

Australia coach Darren Lehmann

Talking Balls

"If he drops me I'll never speak to him again."

Graeme Swann jokes about his new Test captain Alastair Cook

"Critics actually are like girlfriends. They never stop thinking about you."

Rohit Sharma

Q: "What's your favourite animal?"

Steve Waugh: "Merv Hughes."

"He'll bring something to the table. Cluedo, perhaps."

Shane Warne on John Buchanan

THE FUNNIEST CRICKET QUOTES... EVER!

"He's still living off the fact that he coached a team that anyone, even my dog Jerry, could have coached to world domination."
Michael Clarke on John Buchanan

"Contagiously sour. Infectiously dour. He could walk into a room and suck all the joy out of it in five seconds. Just a Mood Hoover. That's how I came to think of him."
Kevin Pietersen on Andy Flower

"Illy [Ray Illingworth] had the man-management skills of Basil Fawlty."
Darren Gough

Talking Balls

"Fred had an unbelievable ability to put six bottles of beer in his mouth at once and down the lot. Quite remarkable."
Michael Vaughan after Andrew Flintoff announced his retirement

"Go on Hedley, you've got him in two minds, he doesn't know whether to hit you for four or six."
Wicket-keeper Arthur Wood to bowler Hedley Verity

"I know why Boycott's bought a house by the sea – so he'll be able to go for a walk on the water."
Fred Trueman

THE FUNNIEST CRICKET QUOTES... EVER!

"I'm not interested in what he has to say. Who is he? He's a nobody."

Kevin Pietersen responds to ex-Australia coach John Buchanan's criticism

"He was saying that there are only two types of batsmen in the world: one is right-handed and one is left-handed."

Rajasthan Royals captain Sanju Samson on bowling coach Lasith Malinga

"Andre Nel is big and raw-boned and I suspect he has the IQ of an empty swimming pool."

Adam Parore

Talking Balls

"Dermot Reeve was so self-obsessed that even on the local nudist beach he only admired himself."
Simon Hughes

"The first time I ever met him he was the same little obnoxious weed that he is now."
Matthew Hayden on Harbhajan Singh

"Chappell was a coward. He needed a crowd around him before he would say anything. He was sour like milk that had been sitting in the sun for a week."
Ian Botham on Ian Chappell

THE FUNNIEST CRICKET QUOTES... EVER!

"If there is an uglier three in the world than Andrew Strauss, Cook and Trott, I don't know of it."
Graeme Swann

"Our Cheese was out there, growing runny in the heat. A Dairylea triangle thinking he was Brie."
Kevin Pietersen on Matt Prior

"I don't know how he's spying on me in the shower."
Steve Smith after coach Justin Langer said he shadow-bats in the shower

Talking Balls

"Geoffrey [Boycott] is the only fellow I've ever met who fell in love with himself at a young age and has remained faithful ever since."
Dennis Lillee

"I'm completely different from Pietersen. He would turn up to the opening of an envelope."
Andrew Flintoff

"I know the dimensions of his a*se from seeing it in close range wicket-keeping behind him for hour after hour after hour."
Adam Gilchrist knows all about Sachin Tendulkar's rear end

THE FUNNIEST CRICKET QUOTES... EVER!

"Srikkanth is a vegetarian. If he swallows a fly, he will be in trouble."

Sunil Gavaskar

David Gower: "Do you want Gatt [Mike Gatting] a foot wider?"

Chris Cowdrey: "No, he'd burst!"

"The schoolyard bully who is also teacher's pet."

Kevin Pietersen on Matt Prior

"Ricky Ponting is back to his old tricks. That bloke would sledge Santa."

Andrew Flintoff

Talking Balls

"You don't get many intelligent fast bowlers for starters, particularly at 19."

Australia T20 captain George Bailey on Pat Cummins

"Samit's had much-publicised problems with the fridge."

Graeme Swann on Samit Patel's England recall

"If I had my way, I would take him to Traitor's Gate and personally hang, draw and quarter him."

Ian Botham on Ray Illingworth

THE FUNNIEST CRICKET QUOTES... EVER!

"Ravi Bopara makes everyone laugh a lot, although it's mainly for always being late or stupid."
Alastair Cook

"Merv is a funny guy, though he would sledge his own mother if he thought it would help the cause."
Gladstone Small on Merv Hughes

"He's a good-looking cat, he's a brilliant athlete, he has a nice family, he's studying law. He can marry one of my daughters."
Justin Langer on Ashton Agar

Talking Balls

"At least I don't wear mascara like Alastair Cook."
Jimmy Anderson

"Built like Tarzan, plays like Jane."
Ricky Ponting on Shaun Tait

"He was the one bloke wetting himself against the quick bowlers."
Mike Atherton on Steve Waugh

"The selectors are full of sh*t."
Chris Lewis after not being picked

THE FUNNIEST CRICKET QUOTES... EVER!

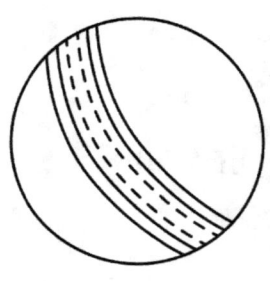

OFF THE PITCH

THE FUNNIEST CRICKET QUOTES... EVER!

"I spent my quarantine getting to know my fiancee."

Australia all-rounder Glenn Maxwell

"Shane Warne's idea of a balanced diet is a cheeseburger in each hand."

Ian Healy

"That means I can drive a flock of sheep through the town centre, drink for free in no less than 64 pubs, and get a lift home with a policeman when I become inebriated. What more could you want?"

Andrew Flintoff after receiving the freedom of Preston

Off The Pitch

"It couldn't have been Gatt. Anything he takes up to his room after nine o'clock, he eats."
Ian Botham on the Mike Gatting barmaid scandal

"The blackcurrant jam tastes of fish to me."
Derek Randall on caviar

"I thought if Rembrandt can do it, why can't I?"
Jack Russell on his new career as an artist

"I am going to spend it with the West Indian women's team."
Chris Gayle on his 33rd his birthday plans

THE FUNNIEST CRICKET QUOTES... EVER!

"I don't think I've actually drunk a beer for 15 years, except a few Guinnesses in Dublin, where it's the law."
Ian Botham

"In my day 58 beers between London and Sydney would have virtually classified you as a teetotaller."
Ian Chappell after David Boon had drunk 58 beers on a team flight to England in 1989. Boon reckoned he was afraid of flying

"Gym. Like dancing, holding hands, queueing. Overrated."
Shane Warne

Off The Pitch

"There are probably Australians stubbing their toes today because of my work."
Stuart Broad laid slabs at a swimming pool in Melbourne aged 17

"I'm so nervous around water I check the bath for sharks."
Michael Clarke after deciding to sail for charity

"When we married I was captain of England, good looking, plenty of money, not a care in the world. Now she is married to a fat old guy, not good looking any more, and no money."
Adam Hollioake on getting into debt

THE FUNNIEST CRICKET QUOTES... EVER!

"I've been in a few adverts but I haven't got the body to be posing about in my underwear like David Beckham."
Stuart Broad

"I'd clear my legs and hit it over cover and they would tell me to go and fetch the ball myself! That's when I said I'm not playing this game."
Virat Kohli is not a fan of golf

"When we go out to field and I'm standing at point, they ask me if I'm going to start eating the grass or not."
Kane Richardson on becoming vegetarian

Off The Pitch

"When I'm back home I honestly, honestly enjoy picking up my dog's sh*t every morning."
Jofra Archer enjoys the simple things while recovering from injury during the Ashes

"I don't ask Kathy to face Michael Holding. So I don't see why I should be changing nappies."
Ian Botham on his responsibilities at home

"After the Ashes victory, I got a lift back to the hotel with Steve Harmison, but I was so carried away with drink and emotion, I spoke Egyptian."
Andrew Flintoff

THE FUNNIEST CRICKET QUOTES... EVER!

"We can hit a moving ball at 90 miles an hour but we can't hit a still ball."

Ben Stokes on his golf game

"I'd rather face Dennis Lillee with a stick of rhubarb than go through that again."

Ian Botham after being cleared of assault charges

Tony Blair: "What do all the f*cking cameras want?"

Matthew Hoggard: "They want a photo, you knobhead."

The England players outside 10 Downing Street after the 2005 Ashes win

Off The Pitch

"Friendship is like p*ssing in your pants, everyone can see it, but only you can feel its true warmth."
Shane Warne

"I'm looking forward to spending more time watching Coronation Street."
Andrew Flintoff loves a soap when he's not playing

"It's a nice town, especially if you don't bring your wives, because then it is a very expensive trip."
Mahela Jayawardene on Kimberley, in South Africa

THE FUNNIEST CRICKET QUOTES... EVER!

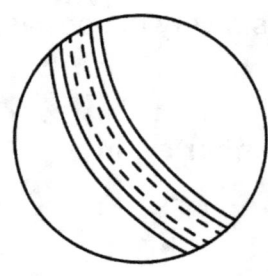

PUNDIT PARADISE

THE FUNNIEST CRICKET QUOTES... EVER!

"Anyone foolish enough to predict the outcome of this match is a fool."
Fred Trueman

"He reminds me of a newly-born giraffe."
Matthew Hayden after Ishant Sharma slipped

"I reckon my mum could have caught that in her pinny!"
Geoffrey Boycott on a dropped catch

"The dew in India is really wet."
Scott Styris

Pundit Paradise

"I have seen fewer hookers in Soho on a Saturday night."

Bob Willis on England's struggles with the short ball against India

"We welcome World Service listeners to the Oval, where the bowler's Holding, the batsman's Willey."

Brian Johnston

"It is important for Pakistan to take wickets if they are going to make inroads into this Australian batting line-up."

Max Walker

THE FUNNIEST CRICKET QUOTES... EVER!

"Imagine if you got him on a triple word score in Scrabble."

David Lloyd on all five first names of Chaminda Vaas

Henry Blofeld: "You'd want Geoffrey Boycott to bat for your life."

Alec Stewart: "It would either be a long life or a slow death."

"If that'd been a hamburger he'd have stopped it."

Bob Willis takes a swipe at a portly Ian Blackwell during a misfield

Pundit Paradise

"How can you have a clash of cultures when you're playing against a country with no culture?"
Former England captain David Gower ahead of the Ashes

"I don't think I've ever seen anything quite like that before – it's the second time it's happened today."
Brian Johnston

"By the time he picks up his broom, the sh*t has hit the ceiling."
Ravi Shastri describes MS Dhoni batting down the lower order

THE FUNNIEST CRICKET QUOTES... EVER!

"If he [Paul Collingwood] was playing outside your house, you'd shut the curtains."
David Lloyd

"And a sedentary seagull flies by."
Brian Johnston

"I would rather I never have to see him again but unfortunately we work fairly close together."
Ian Chappell on Ian Botham

"If I was on 99 and at the other end and you got out, I'd hit you with my bat."
Geoffrey Boycott to Matthew Hoggard

Pundit Paradise

"An interesting morning, full of interest."

Jim Laker

"If the tension here was a block of Cheddar cheese, you could cut it with a knife."

Henry Blofeld

"The hallmark of a great captain is the ability to win the toss at the right time."

Richie Benaud

"This series has been swings and pendulums all the way through."

Trevor Bailey

THE FUNNIEST CRICKET QUOTES... EVER!

"It is now possible they can get the impossible score they first thought possible."

Christopher Martin-Jenkins

"I think the batsman's strategy will be to make runs and not get out."

Richie Benaud

"The other advantage England have got when Phil Tufnell is bowling is that he isn't fielding."

Ian Chappell

"I've never got to the bottom of streaking."

Jonathan Agnew

Pundit Paradise

"I don't think he expected it, and that's what caught him unawares."

Trevor Bailey

"England have nothing to lose here, apart from this Test match."

David Lloyd

"Three bad days does not mean you're a bad team overnight."

Paul Collingwood

"And Ian Greig's on eight, including two fours."

Jim Laker

THE FUNNIEST CRICKET QUOTES... EVER!

"There were congratulations and high sixes all round."

Richie Benaud

"A few years ago England would have struggled to beat the Eskimos."

Ian Botham

"On the first day, Logie decided to chance his arm and it came off."

Trevor Bailey

"It's tough for a natural hooker to give it up."

Ian Chappell

Pundit Paradise

"More brains in a pork pie."

Geoffrey Boycott on Kevin Pietersen

"There's Neil Harvey standing at leg slip with his legs wide apart, waiting for a tickle."

Brian Johnston

"England might now be the favourites to draw this match."

Vic Marks

"Ray Illingworth has just relieved himself at the Pavilion End."

Brian Johnston

THE FUNNIEST CRICKET QUOTES... EVER!

"It's a catch he would have caught 99 times out of 1,000."

Henry Blofeld

"Sean Pollock there, a carbon copy of his dad. Except he's a bit taller and he's got red hair."

Trevor Bailey

"There were no scores below single figures."

Richie Benaud

"There's only one head bigger than Tony Greig's and that's Birkenhead."

Fred Trueman

Pundit Paradise

"Where's your hanky, love?"

Danny Morrison when a tearful RCB fan watched her team collapse

"He played a cut so late as to be positively posthumous."

John Arlott

"This is the sort of pitch which literally castrates a bowler."

Trevor Bailey

"To stay in, you've got to not get out."

Geoffrey Boycott

"If they made a film of my life, I think they should get George Clooney to play me."

THE FUNNIEST FOOTBALL QUOTES... EVER!

"Mario woke up this morning with a hardening – in his thigh!"

by Gordon Law

www.ingramcontent.com/pod-product-compliance
Lightning Source LLC
Chambersburg PA
CBHW050300120526
44590CB00016B/2433